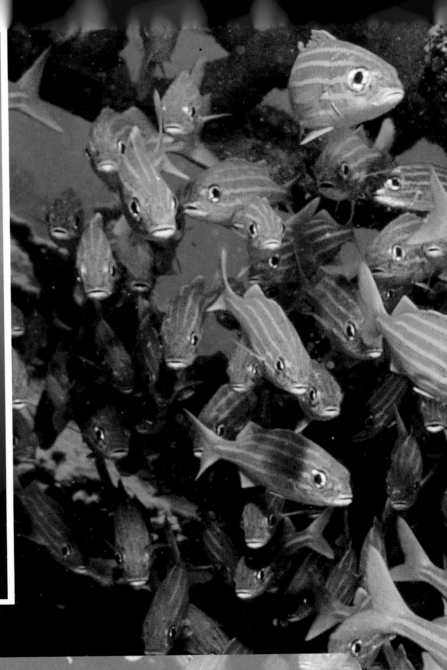

The waters of the Caribbean Sea are warm and clear. On the surface, everything appears peaceful. But just below, rising from the bottom of the sea, there is a very busy place. It is the underwater community of the coral reef.

Habitats

CORAL REEF

GARY W. DAVIS

ℭℙ Children's Press

A Division of Grolier Publishing
New York London Hong Kong Sydney
Danbury, Connecticut

Created and Developed by The Learning Source

Designed by Josh Simons

Acknowledgments: We would like to thank the people at Tom Stack & Associates and the other organizations who provided technical assistance with this project. Their help is greatly appreciated.

All illustrations by Arthur John L'Hommedieu

Photo Credits: Brian Parker/Tom Stack & Associates: 1, 2 (background), 4 -9, 11 (inset), 13-14, 16, 19, 22-23, 28-29, 32; Cindy Garoutte/PDS/Tom Stack: 20; Ed Robinson/Tom Stack: 21; Larry Lipsky/Tom Stack: cover, 3, 12, 15, 18, 20, 24, 25 (right), back cover; Mike Bacon/Tom Stack: 10, 17, 25 (left); Randy Morse/Tom Stack: 11 (background).

Library of Congress Cataloging-in-Publication Data

Davis, Gary, 1946-
     Coral reef / by Gary Davis.
        p. cm. — (Habitats)
     Summary: Text and photographs reveal the busy undersea life of a Caribbean Sea coral reef.
     ISBN 0-516-20711-3 (lib. bdg.) 0-516-20375-4 (pbk.)
     1. Coral reef ecology — Juvenile literature. 2. Coral reef biology — Juvenile literature. 3. Coral reef ecology — Caribbean Sea — Juvenile literature. 4. Coral reef biology — Caribbean Sea — Juvenile literature. [1. Coral reefs and islands. 2. Coral reef ecology. 3. Ecology. 4. Coral reef animals. 5. Caribbean Sea.] I. Title. II. Series: Habitats (Children's Press).
QH541.5.C7D34 1997
577.7'89—dc21
96-51021

                                              CIP
                                            AC

Printed in China.
9 10 11 12 13 R 19 18 17

The coral reef often provides the only food and shelter for miles around. So the reef becomes crowded—the center of life for hundreds of different kinds of plants and animals. Day and night, something is always going on.

Most coral reefs are made up of different colonies, or parts. One colony might look like a strange plant or a deer antler or even a giant brain. No matter what kind it is, all coral colonies have something in common. Each is made by tiny sea animals called coral polyps (POL-ups).

Elkhorn Coral

Brain Coral

Fire Coral

Pillar Coral

Coral polyps take calcium from sea water to build limestone houses around their bodies. When a polyp dies, its house remains. All colonies, even this rounded brain coral, are made from the limestone homes of many thousands of coral polyps.

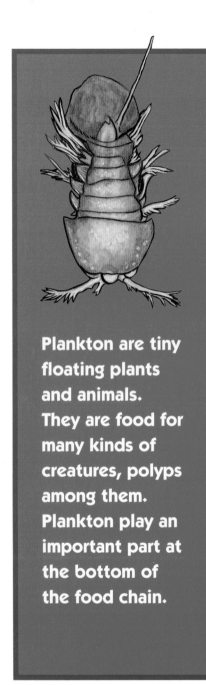

Plankton are tiny floating plants and animals. They are food for many kinds of creatures, polyps among them. Plankton play an important part at the bottom of the food chain.

Outside its house, each tiny polyp looks like a strange flower with a mouth. Arms, called tentacles, surround the mouth. On each tentacle are stingers for catching any plankton that might float by.

Brand-new colonies start from fertilized coral eggs. Then, like budding plants, colonies of coral grow at their tips or edges. The colonies branch outward and upward, very, very slowly. It can take 50 years or more for a coral colony to grow only 3 feet (91 centimeters).

All kinds of living things exist on or around the reef. Some, such as sea anemones, are actually attached to the reef. To catch food, anemones wave their stinging tentacles at small creatures swimming by.

Other animals, such as these giant sea fans and sponges, attach themselves to the reef, too. And plants, seaweed and algae among them, also grow right on the reef, wherever they can find enough light and room.

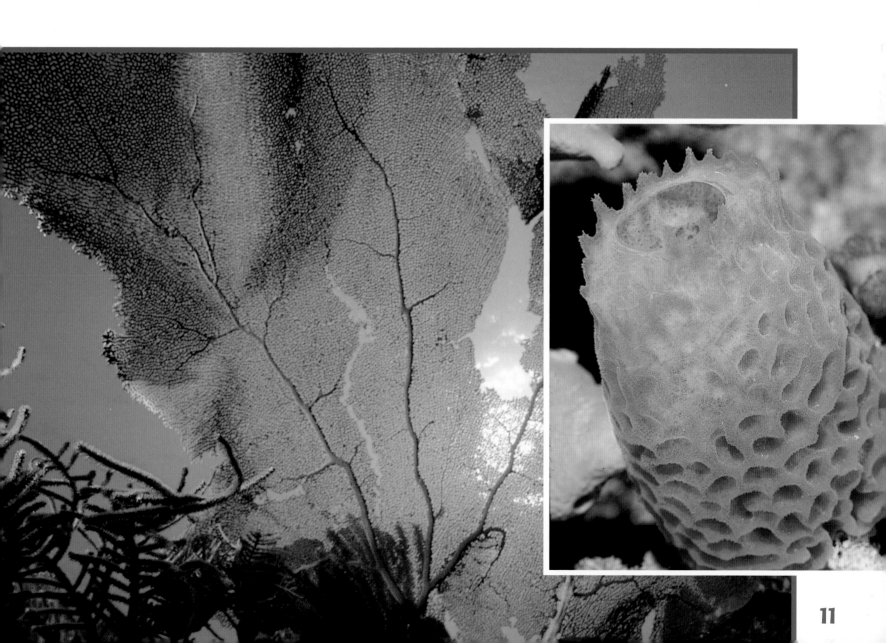

Most reef animals are awake during the day. They have good eyes and are able to see different colors. This is important because color often sends messages from one creature to another. The bold stripes on these butterfly fish, for example, warn other butterfly fish that a territory is taken.

The bright colors of an angelfish help it find a mate. But bright colors can also be a warning that a fish is poisonous.

Camouflage lets creatures blend in with their background. This can help them get food. It can also protect them from becoming food for someone else.

A flat-bodied flounder is nearly invisible against the sandy bottom. Any hunting fish could easily miss it, even at close range.

This hungry scorpion fish looks just like part of the reef. It will easily be able to gobble up many unsuspecting creatures. Trumpetfish can change color to blend into different backgrounds. And their long, skinny bodies look like branches of coral.

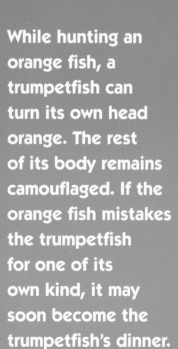

While hunting an orange fish, a trumpetfish can turn its own head orange. The rest of its body remains camouflaged. If the orange fish mistakes the trumpetfish for one of its own kind, it may soon become the trumpetfish's dinner.

The blue and black stripes on cleaner fish act as a sign saying, "We are cleaners. Our job is to keep you healthy." Many reefs have cleaning stations where customers wait patiently in line.

Some reef animals work together as partners. Little goby fish clean the bodies of much larger fish. In turn, the gobies eat what they find as they clean. So, while one partner gets a free meal, the other stays clean and healthy.

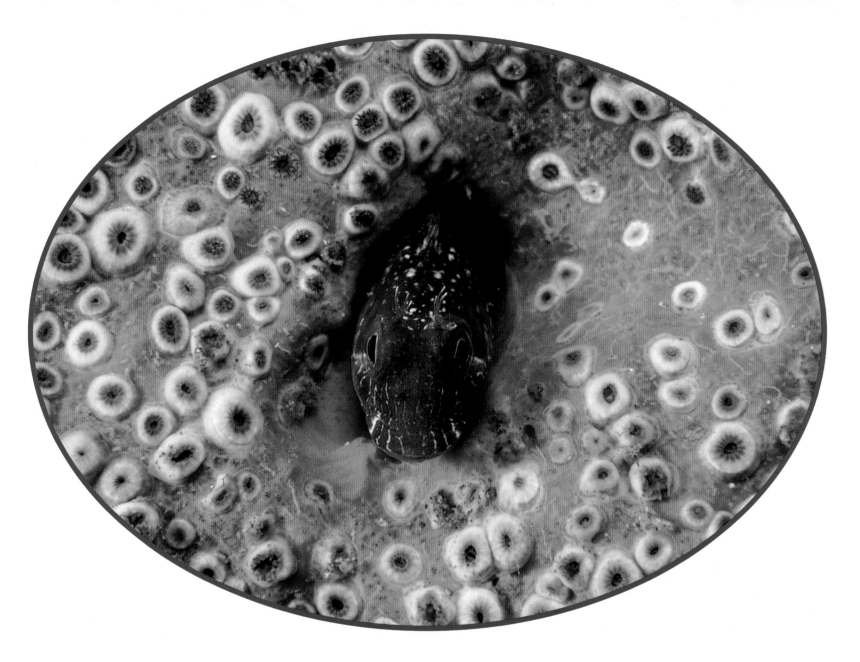

This seaweed blenny fish spends most of its time
inside the tunnels and chambers of sponges. Other small
fish live safely beneath spiny sea urchins. The little fish
are protected. But nobody knows what the sponges and
sea urchins get in return.

Many fish eat in odd ways. A parrotfish eats plants that grow on coral. But when its scraperlike teeth go after plants, the fish often takes in chunks of coral as well. So, as the parrotfish eats the plants, it noisily grinds chunks of coral into tiny pieces of sand.

A sea horse, perhaps the oddest fish of all, holds onto the reef with its tail. There it waits, using its straw-shaped mouth to suck in lots of passing shrimp.

The sea horse is most unusual because the male gives birth to the young. After the female lays her eggs, it is the male's job to keep them in his special body pouch until hatching time.

It is twilight, and day is fading into night. Now many larger fish come to hunt on the reef. Quickly, the smaller daytime fish swim for cover just as groupers, silvery barracudas, and sharks move in.

The hunters can easily see movement and shape in the dimly lit waters. These fierce creatures quickly eat their fill and leave. For a few moments, just after sunset, the reef is calm and silent. But then . . .

. . . all the night creatures burst onto the scene. How different everything looks now! Coral polyps, after hiding all day in their stony houses, put out their flowing tentacles to feed.

Featherduster and tube worms also come out. Their feathery arms reach out to catch food and take in oxygen.

Crabs and spiny lobsters leave their safe hiding places on the reef to scavenge for food.

Many night fish come out, too. Squirrelfish and grunts feed near the reef. Because it is dark, these creatures do not depend on their eyesight. Instead, they use their senses of touch, taste, and smell to survive.

With its keen sense of smell, a fierce moray eel hunts down an octopus. The suction cups on the octopus's eight arms, or tentacles, give it a fine sense of taste and touch. But these do not help against the moray.

Suddenly, the moray's strong jaws bite into one of the octopus's tentacles. But all is not lost. The octopus simply breaks off its trapped arm and squirts out a heavy cloud of ink. The ink blocks the eel's sense of smell, and the octopus escapes. Before long, the octopus will grow a new tentacle.

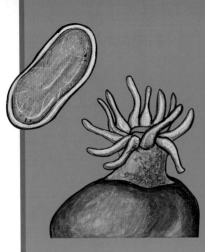

A fertilized coral egg hatches into a larva, called a planula. It drifts for several days before attaching itself to a hard, clean surface. The planula then changes into a polyp and begins to build a limestone house.

At last, the night creatures have eaten and gone off to rest. In the safety of the calm, dark waters, a coral polyp quietly releases many eggs. Perhaps one of the eggs will start a new colony. Someday it may even grow to the size of this pillar coral.

The night is finally over. Soon, dawn comes to the reef. Coral polyps pull in their swaying tentacles as sharks and other hunters swim through the dim light.

Night creatures sleep hidden beneath coral ledges. Day creatures are just waking. A new day is beginning for the many, many creatures living on and around the coral reef.

More About

Moray Eel, Page 3:
A moray eel will attack almost anything that gets too close. Oddly though, a little cleaner fish can go inside a moray's mouth and clean its teeth without coming to any harm.

Fire Coral, Page 9:
Fire coral is not named for its color, but for the fiery sting of its tiny tentacles.

Carribean Sea, Page 4:
Carribean water is clearer than colder northern waters because there are fewer tiny organisms in it. That is why so many creatures depend on the coral reef for food.

Sea Fan, Page 11:
Sea fans are really soft corals. They have flexible skeletons that let them bend, like trees, without breaking.

Coral Polyp, Page 8:
Tiny microscopic plants live inside a coral polyp's body. These plants provide food for the polyp and help it to make limestone.

Butterfly Fish, Page 12:
With a mouth shaped like a pair of long-nosed pliers, a butterfly fish pokes into the reef looking for food. Some of its favorites are worms, tiny shrimp, and tender coral polyps.

This Habitat

Scorpion Fish, Page 15:
Any sea creature that bumps into a scorpion fish is probably in big trouble. That's because the spines of a scorpion fish are coated with deadly poison.

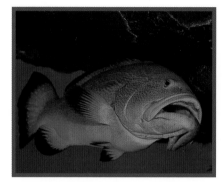

Grouper, Page 20:
Giant groupers have been said to swallow divers whole and then spit them out! It seems that the big fish don't like the taste of the divers' wetsuits.

Parrotfish, Page 18:
To get a safe night's sleep, a parrotfish wraps itself in a sticky cocoon. The cocoon seals off the fish's scent, protecting it from hungry enemies.

Squirrelfish, Page 25:
Squirrelfish and their relatives have been around since the time of the dinosaurs. They have primitive eyes that can only see motion.

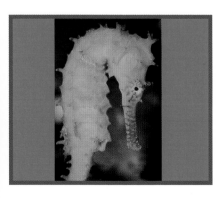

Sea Horse, Page 19:
A sea horse has no stomach and cannot store food. So, it must eat constantly. A young sea horse may eat as many as 3,500 shrimp a day.

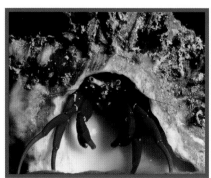

Hermit Crab, Page 32
Hermit crabs never build their own houses. Instead, they find shells abandoned by other sea creatures and move right in. When a crab grows too big for one shell, it just finds another.